# Ways to Thrive and Survive in Corporate America

---

## A compilation of our best practices based on real world experiences

Written by

Angela Findley

Co-Authored by

Scott Findley

2

# Contents

This book is not for the faint of heart, you will actually have to ask for help, sometimes that help will come from the most unlikely of places.

## Introduction

There...now that the legal stuff is out of the way, it is time to think outside of the box. In today's hard economic times, many individuals find themselves in unfamiliar surroundings.

Regardless, if you have a degree or not, your career is not dead. You are not doomed or destined to live in a dungeon filing papers.

There is a whole world available to you as long as you have the drive, determination, and fortitude to push your boundaries. Keep an eye out for the jobs that you would have never considered before. Most of these career opportunities are outside of the normal industries, or standard companies that you are used to.

One night my husband Scott and I sat talking about the freelance articles I was writing, and my novel that will be out soon. Then he suggested something that started this completely crazy book.

"What if we wrote about our jobs?" I knew that no one wants to read stories of paper pushing, and filing. So as I sat there with a perplexed look on my face.

"You know, how we made it." That was it! A book on how we had both became professionally successful and respected in our fields.

We had both achieved a lot in our careers; we traveled extensively, headed up teams, and organizations, became Project Management Professionals. We had several promotions and more times than not, we were looked to, as the "go to" people.

However, with most people today, jobs move, and companies downsize. Now...you can sit back, complain, and argue that it should have been someone else.

Stop yourself; it will never be the best time to get laid off. Learn this one lesson early; no one is irreplaceable.

Neither my husband nor I had ever been one of those people who were content with doing the same task repeatedly. Nor were we the people who could impede persons' daily routines with telemarketing. Therefore, we both converged on Corporate America, starting at the bottom and working diligently up the rungs of the ladder.

Scott had worked his way up through Retail Warehousing, and I through the Manufacturing arena. Both had their benefits, and taught us the closed loop that comes with any and we mean, any business.

If you are sitting there, saying my business has nothing to do with

Manufacturing or Retail; in the simplest terms, you are lying to yourself. Every task in a business deals with supply and demand.

You may not produce a 'thingy', but you produce a service or distribute 'thingies'. Again, supply and demand, and everyone is a customer.

Now I hear you brainy types saying, "All of the work I do is behind the scenes, it's up to the big guys to sell the stuff." Without you, there would be nothing to sell. Even the lowly filers, have some of the most important jobs, in this crazy world we call work.

This book has nothing to do with staying 'under the radar', and or 'getting by' or being successful because of other peoples work. Every success we have had has been because of hard work and a willingness to learn.

We have been very fortunate as well, both having good managers in our past. The ones we hold in the highest regard were the managers who looked past title and education. Looking for the expertise and fortitude to get the job done, these individuals are the ones who keep this completely crazy corporate world spinning.

To them, you know who you are...we Thank You.

However, with anything in life, we've also had Managers who were threatened by our knowledge. Not because we did anything bad or illegal, but because we had more working and technical information than they did.

As throughout life, there are the people you can trust and rely on, and then there are others, who are takers only. No matter what and we mean this, "These people will never change!" Get away from them as quickly as possible; they are like paths of destruction for your career.

Once the takers have been identified, stay away from them. They will hurt your career and public standing, because generally they are as tarnished as their practices.

Believe me when we say we have been through our share of trials and tribulations, which not only the non-degreed, but extensively degreed individuals all deal with.

Some experiences have been, being downsized, a company moving several states away, and multiple mergers and buy-outs. Through it all we still kept going, and did well for ourselves.

Along the pages of this book are tidbits by which we live, they have worked for us, proven only by our forty plus years combined in the business world. It was not

easy however; we survived it all
and built a nice life. Good luck
and we hope this helps.

*Words to never, ever use:*

*There is no place for an ax, in the workplace. Unless you work for a lumberjack supplier, the word is ask.*

*Hygiene: Keep it clean, enough said.*

*Try keeping "UM" to a minimum in the workplace. Try saying instead "I don't know." Alternatively "I can find out for you", or even "That's a good question".*

## <u>Bachelors Degree or equivalent -</u>
## <u>Words not to be afraid of</u>

'Degreed or not degreed, that is the question.'

Both have their downfalls when looking for a new job.

For instance, you have a Masters Degree in business, worked for a local mega company, and then the turn...You are now out of work, the local economy is bottoming out, and there are no 'white collar' jobs anywhere.

You have never been one to turn away from a hard day of work, and you love working with wood.

A local furniture manufacture has an opening for a wood carver, decent wage. "Yes...I got this!"

"No, I'm sorry but you are overqualified."

Regardless if you saw yourself working there until retirement, they see you as an unstable and short-term employee.

Now, same local mega company, different employee: A lowly non-degreed assembler who knows the operating system inside and out, because they worked in multiple areas over a longer tenure.

They apply for a management role, and get it.

Why?

They have no sense of entitlement, or vanity that comes with title. In addition, they are more flexible when it comes to learning and are generally more eager to do the right thing.

Not, that they are demigods who never make mistakes, however, they do have firsthand experience of what can happen, if the right thing is not done.

Bachelors degree or equivalent, believe what they are saying, when they write it, they mean it. Most companies are required to be Equal Opportunity Employers.

Now, you are not going to be performing brain surgery and

they are not going to hand over the keys to any rockets.

However, there is still a great appreciation for acquired experience, regardless of your educational background. So go for it, the worst you can be told is no.

The best time for anyone to look for a job is when you have one. If you do this, you will not feel pressured to accept less than you are worth; even without a degree, you have skills, which make you valuable.

List out your skills and see where it takes you, then go for the job that highlights your already existing capabilities. Only you can be the judge of your abilities, please be honest with yourself. It is not always pretty but it has to happen.

Play to those attributes, it will help move you forward in your career path. Think about your personality and what you enjoy doing; do not go after an analyst job if you hate lists.

If you are a people person, going after an entry-level job in a sales office, or customer service, would be a good start.

If you are the kind of person that knows the latest operating system inside and out; because you played with it on some obscure website, in its beta phase. That makes you a great fit for Informational Technologies, or a consultant.

However, be honest, to not only your prospective employer, but yourself as well.

Fiddling with it for a minute, and knowing the ins and outs of the program, are two completely different things.

Remember in today's society of buzzwords and influential speak, your vocabulary will also help you get the job.

Instead of being a gas station attendant, you could describe yourself as a customer service agent, or retail specialist. This is again a broad term, but do not sell yourself short, you did those things!

You have been the face of your company; they have paid you to do the right thing, so keep it up.

When asked, during the interview process if you have any experience with problem resolution.

Instead of saying 'not really', or 'that you had to override the cash register to give the correct sale price.' Instead, say, 'I was a key contributor to customer service satisfaction and issue resolution.'

You could easily hand off an irate customer to the manager, but take advantage of these occurrences, and the experience it will give you.

Please do not take these word for word; the idea is that no matter how bad you believe your job is, it has given you skills that equates somewhere in the business world.

Change the situation to a manufacturing facility; instead of the "wrong price", 'The projects components cannot be located.', or 'The data file is not in the correct partitioned drive.', or 'The delivery did not make it in on time.'

All of these are examples of issue identification and problem resolution.

Again, these are examples and not to be taken word for word, they are meant to get you thinking at your job from other angles.

If you sold anything and paid attention, you understand the principles of supply and demand, purchasing, and accounts payable and receivables. What degree of knowledge, that is for you to decide.

If you interview well, and voice your willingness to learn, most companies will give you a shot.

You will not be heading up any teams to start, but once you can prove that you know what you are talking about; you can be given more responsibilities and opportunities.

Do you work in a service industry and like it? You may be in one of the best positions over anyone.

There are quite a few companies, who promote from within. You know you have heard of crazy salaries made by these people who have worked their ways up the ranks. No one is lying; these organizations pay them well for their hard work.

## Appearance - Even if your broke

We have all been there searching for a job, while working at the neighborhood restaurant or gas station, where the uniform consists of blue jeans and a t-shirt. Then along comes your big break, the company you applied to, calls, and asks for an interview.

Just because you do not have the immediate gear or cash to go out and buy a suit, do not worry.

Do not be proud if you have zero cash, your friends and family can help. Borrow a pair of khaki pants from a friend and a nice button down shirt from Dad.  Ladies slacks, or skirt and a blouse.

If you only have a few bucks to buy clothes, be the best bargain shopper you can be. It may take more time, but you can walk out of stores with two outfits, sans shoes, for thirty bucks.

Color blind? Not a problem, ask for help. It is easy and you never know what opportunities can arise from a simple conversation. *See Networking and Public Interaction*

When getting dressed for an interview or maintaining your everyday ensemble for the workplace. Remember to dress appropriately for your actual size. There should be in no way any; cramming, stuffing, grunting, stretching, or ripping.

Nothing flashy or audacious and no jumpsuits, leisure suits, ruffled pirate shirts, headbands, bandanas, tennis shoes, etc. If you look silly, people will not take you seriously.

Simple dressing etiquette also applies, shirts tucked in, belt, etc. As long as your clothes are clean, pressed or wrinkle free, and free of holes or major tatters, you should be ok.

Women, please do not show off your lacy undergarments, expose too much flesh, or strain the buttons on your blouse. Your skirt length in the workplace should be judged, by the bend over rule. If you are flashing people when you bend over, get a longer skirt.

New to town with no friends or family, there are organizations out there that will help you.

Check with your local library or government offices for listings. Find these places and check them out before you receive the call for the interview.

Being prepared is just as important as looking the part, and putting off an interview is never a good option. If you are looking to get more, you have to be willing to put forth the effort and forethought.

## Interviewing – A necessary evil

Going through the interview process is nerve-wracking at best; however, you have to rise above the jitters. Most jobs are won because of knowledge, personality, and confidence.

Firstly, let's begin with what not to do...

When you get to the business for your interview, before you even get out of the car, turn your phone off.

Yes off, your phone may be your personal assistant and has everything you could possibly need in an interview. However, this is not the time or place for technology.

Have your information printed out ahead of time. (I.e. resume, references with contact information, etc.)

You do not want to have to promise to send the information; you want to be prepared. Showing that you have the forethought to provide the necessary information will show your commitment.

"Ok but why turn the phone off, I could hit silence or vibrate. No big deal, right?"

Wrong! Think about walking through a vast technology and toy store, with dozens of signs stating, "Try-me!"

What do we do? We push every button we can get our hands on... What makes you think, you would not be checking it while you wait...do not do it, it shows impatience.

Next scenario, you silence your phone but inadvertently placed your keys in the same pocket.

We have all been there, 'The accidental dial!'

The worst thing that could happen is that either someone answers or now you have to scramble to hang-up. Alternatively, the person on the other end realizes the mistake and hangs up.

Either way your phone will be going off or alerting you to the call. Not good, no matter whom you are...just shut it off.

"Ok now for the touchy feely stuff, yes it has to be done...sorry."

We already know that our responses and body language are the keys to getting us a job. What that means; that without even stepping foot inside the new business, we are already on edge.

Do not give into these internal reactions, you have to keep calm and collected during the process.

You can beat yourself up later, for now focus on the moment, and always stay tuned into what the other person is saying.

When your interviewer asks you if you have any questions, ask questions!

Have these written down along with your other documentation.

This shows the other person that you are proactive and know what you need from the company as well as what you are willing to offer.

The interview process is rough enough to pop out a few grays and fill your mind with paranoia and self-doubt. Pride is what makes it difficult for us to go willingly just to be judged. It is tough, but you have to get through it.

So why does everyone freak out? What is the worst that could happen? All you can be told is no.

No, such a simple word, yet a word that deflates egos, and ends dreams.

If you allow it, do not be one of those people who take no for an answer, it just means no for right now.

You can be told no for a multitude of reasons. Remember it is mostly because someone else is a better fit for the job.

If not, See *Nepotism – It's real, you have to cope!*

## New job New Company – What worked for us.

Research your prospective employer; most state governments have offices where you can use their computers for job listings, web searches and resume help. Check with your local libraries and/or government listings.

If the company you are looking to work for is small, talk to the locals. You can generally get a feeling from the community if it is a good place to work or not.

Big enough company to have a website? Check it out; the information provided will help you. Go to their FAQ section as well as the About Us tabs. This information could benefit you during your interview process.

Get behind the mission statements, and understand where they are coming from. The company's outlook and philosophy will be a good determiner, if this is the right one for you.

If the businesses stand point conflicts with your own personal opinions, philosophies, or beliefs in any way, do not apply.

You will not change the working environment; you being the passionate voice of reason for your beliefs, will only help you lose your job faster.

Including, but not limited to, you being miserable and it is just not worth it. Jobs are equal to the amount of fish in the sea, there are many out there.

Through the interview process whatever you do, be honest. You may believe you are a good liar, but they know. If it sounds too good to be true it probably is, so don't try and spoof your way through an interview.

Be honest and let your interviewer know what you bring

to the table. Knowing your strengths and voicing a willingness to learn, has done wonders for many a career.

If you do not get the job, you were going after, thank the person for the follow-up, and let them know of your willingness to work for them.

Let them know you are still looking, and to keep you in mind for future jobs.

Generally, if you interviewed well, but you skills didn't fit the bill, you are not dead in the water.

Most interviewers take notes, and will recommend you for another position, or tell you to keep an eye on the website.

Do it and if you get an interview, send a thank you note to your first interviewer. Not the same person, it doesn't matter, soon they could be your peer; and will be more apt to help you, once you get in the door.

## New job within the same company – Don't slow down now!

Same rules apply; even if you work in the mailroom, you are responsible for so much more than delivering interoffice memos.

If your company is big enough to have a mailroom, you are in a great position to get involved and learn the business.

Take the time to get to know and learn about the people you are servicing. The roles they play in the grand scheme of things will help you in the most diverse ways imaginable.

Some of the greatest wins in the working world have been due to successes in underling roles, or in the trenches, as they are called.

Starting out on the bottom rung of the corporate ladder is not a bad way to go. You then learn as you go, and get the gradual exposure that is necessary to get ahead.

Be the person who is unwilling to sit idle. Instead fiddle, not that kind of fiddling, the kind where you open a program that you have never used before and see what it does.

Play with Programs, Check out the Operating System, read the companies Standard Operating Procedures. Ingraining yourself within the company will give you a huge advantage. See: *Office Programs – Have fun don't worry*

Ok, you do not have access to the gadgetry yet? Ask for something to do.

If you get your tasks done, do not wait to be checked up on. Double check your work, and move on, ask if there are other things that need doing.

Heads up on this one, it could include filing, cleaning, or any other undone petty task that is lingering around.

Your eagerness and efficiency are all attributes that get you recognized, as long as you do it properly.

No one is going to promote you, if your reports contain massive errors, or misspelled words being more prevalent than the correct verbiage. *See: Never hide a mistake!*

These may seem like silly moot points, however if you cannot be bothered to spell a word correctly, how can you be bothered to run your team effectively?

Bottom line, being conscience of your outer interactions can make or break you.

## Water cooler Discussions: What not to talk about

Your friends are your friends and your colleagues are your colleagues, remember that. There are times to be open and upfront to your colleagues, and there are times not to be.

If you spent your vacation partying your way across Europe, ensuring you hit every beer garden along your route. Keep it to yourself, instead describe your trip in a broad sweep of your verbal paintbrush, and be noncommittal; "The sites in Europe were amazing! The people were so nice, and the food was Fantastic!"

Even if it was the worst vacation you have ever taken, keep the negativity out of the workplace. Commiserating with your pals is fine, they understand you, and your boss does not.

No one wants to hear complaining. Let me repeat that, "No One, wants to hear complaining!"

Complaining comes in many forms and it is up to you to make sure, that you do not complain. Once you have, you may not be able to undo the damage that procrastination or complaints have done to you.

You could become 'blackballed'. Which is an oxymoron if you think about it, to sink the blackball is to win, however not in the workplace!

Complaining about your peers, customers, suppliers or any other person you encounter, is a definite no-no! What you are doing is showing your leaders that you are not mature enough to be a valuable member of the team atmosphere.

Frustration is very acceptable, but only in small doses. Say your shipment was moved forward in the delivery schedule and you now have to give up your tickets to your favorite band. Go ahead, vent. However, vent once and move on, anything more makes you sound like a whiner.

If you are always the person throwing your hands up in the air, you are using it TOO MUCH!

If you act like that all the time, it is no longer frustration. It has turned to negativity and an unwillingness to participate. That may not be how you feel, but that is how people will perceive you.

Instead of "That will never work!", try "Will the 'change' have an effect to the current procedures, or plan?" Talk through the change and ask questions. Remember only ask the questions that are relevant to the current discussion.

Do not ask how this will affect you directly. *See Business – Don't be that...!*

Doing so will bring you into the teamwork fold. Use your experience to guide your questions and your team to make the situation work for everyone.

Remember there are no bad questions, only mistakes made by not asking the question.

*Quips & Quandaries:*

*Never underestimate the power
of Networking.*

*Perception is reality, no matter if
it is true or not.*

*Keep personal items to a
minimum. A few personal knick-
knacks are good; however, a
shrine to your favorite rocker or
sports team doesn't look good.*

## E-mail – The Silent Killer

We've all seen it happen, unfortunately it has directly happened to others of us,' Reply All'. If you can find the recall function quick enough, you are lucky.

Therefore, the best advice that can be given; is to double check, no matter the dead line. Double check that the content makes sense, also who will be receiving it, many a corporate deal has gone south, due to a miss-sent e-mail.

Example: "Your shipment fell off the truck and disintegrated after being run over by a snow-plow." What do you do?

Firstly, do not panic! Secondly, regain your composure and think logically who should be involved in the initial crisis. This is not the time or place to send e-mails to everyone throughout the company.

Your direct leadership can direct that traffic, you focus on the things you have control over.

Many a career has ended because of over advertising a problem via e-mail. E-mail has its place; there is also a time and place to pick-up the phone, or meet with the person face to face.

People can be influenced more easily if there is verbal or face-to-face communications. Either option is more appropriate in the business world, anything is better than being berated by a mountain of e-mails.

In today's world of technology and social networks, people are in constant communication. Do not count on the fact that your e-mail made it safely through all filters, unless you have an established stable rapport.

However just as you 'have a job to do'; the person on the other end of that connection does as well. Give them the time to reply, do not double check that they are working on it.

If you do let your e-mail wait, a day is standard, unless you need information by a deadline. In that case, pick up a phone and ask the question. Most professionals have intimate knowledge of what is on their plates and should be able to give you the answers quickly.

The one thing that many people can attest too is that e-mail is impersonal. It has no empathy check; it is only as personable as you are. Do not make the classic mistake of trying to use sarcasm in an e-mail.

Try doing it yourself. Type a sarcastic message for yourself, save the message on your desktop. Read it later.

Now say, the person on the other end of that message had a bad day, things were going wrong. Nothing they touched was right, now they get your e-mail. BOOM!

Now this is not how you meant for your correspondence to read, but all they read was a curt e-mail, that did not help their day.

Take each e-mail as an opportunity to build bridges, and networks. Always start out with a 'Good Day, Hope all is well, Good Morning, etc.' and a salutation at the end. 'All the Best, Thank you, appreciate your help, etc.'

These little items could make someone's day, and if you have brightened someone's mood, they will remember you!

Getting ahead is sometimes as simple as sending a follow-up e-mail. Not only is it a great professional courtesy, but no one is going to turn down appreciation or recognition for their work. It also sends the message that you give credit where credit is due.

## Never hide a mistake

Double check?"  Yes, double check! People make mistakes, almost never intentionally. However, they happen and you do not want to be that person.

The first thing you should do is double check your notes, and make sure you are giving the person what they have asked for. Re-read through your work, make sure it reads properly, also that the content is clear and concise

"OK, I've double checked everything. Can I move on, already?"

Sure go ahead, but when a colleague stops by and points out a screaming error in your data. Do not freak out!

Stop...take a deep breath...exhale slowly.

Now fix your mistake and resend the presentation with a heartfelt apology. Yep, you have to admit you screwed up!

Ok, now that you are done running and screaming; about how you could never do such things.

Look back on the situation and take your lumps; you will actually come out better in the end. Instead of letting the mistake go, correcting it will put you in a great place.

Instead of peers criticizing you behind your back, you will be looked at, as a valuable member of the team. Sounds crazy, but it gives credence to you being someone who believes in doing the right thing.

Remember those takers?

Yes, they work there too. You will have the people who try to push their blame onto you. Take it...yes, take it. At least while you are in the meeting.

Outside the meeting, they are fair game. Don't be pushed around because you feel inadequate about your education or title, if you were in the right, say so.

Pull them aside afterwards, once and only after you have settled down. Then calmly tell them if they push their issues on to you again, you will escalate it up the proper channels.

If you are always the person who has been the most honest,

correct, and forthright, sit back and enjoy the show!

The 'takers' will show their true colors soon enough, and will hose up their own careers. Many a corporate bully has thrown their colleagues under the proverbial bus. Don't give in to the drama, and take the high road, all the while being prepared to take them out of the game.

'The SOB did it again!' Have your proof ready and be clear, concise, and correct. Again, don't whine! See *Water cooler Discussions: What not to talk about.*

Ok, now that we've told you how to avoid mistakes; here is a situation where you will probably make tons of mistakes. Learn from those mistakes, and try to minimize the impact to your work.

The one thing that will set you apart from the rest, is your ability to make the call.

If you are faced with a decision that needs to be made, do not wait for someone to empower you. Make the call! You can always change your mind, or change directions, but do not wait for others to do it for you.

You will show that you have what it takes to lead teams. If you screw it up, make sure you only make the mistake once. Multiple mistakes over and over will lead your career to that ugly place.

Yep, save that for the other yahoo, who deserves to be there.

*More dos and don'ts:*

*Effect & Affect they are different, research it first before you try to sound brainy.*

*Words to never, ever use: Irregardless is not a word, the word is regardless look it up!*

*Supposedly – hearing this simple word butchered is terrible, it is d not b as in supposebly (Really it is not a word!) .*

## Networking and Public Interaction

Broadening your knowledge helps you, even if that information is based off someone else's career or expertise. If most people are asked to discuss their knowledge, jobs, fields, or organizations, they will jump at the opportunity. Do not pass it up, listen, learn, and ask questions.

You may not believe this now, but sometime, somewhere that information is going to be helpful. All jobs are structured the same way, supply and demand. Eventually most local employers reach out within their communities to get contractors.

Understand, you do not have to spend every waking hour on the internet or spend your hard-earned money, schmoozing your potential network friends.

However, a professional courtesy or referral goes a long way. Handing off someone's business card and telling them to drop your name at the business, establishes you as a stable professional and a person who is loyal.

Loyalty can earn you many things, from promotions, shining references, free services, or referrals of your own. You may never get anything from a network connection; those losses are just to be expected.

Your colleague got a promotion, even if it is the one you went after, be the bigger person and say congratulations.

If you take rejection in stride, you will be far more apt to get the next one. If you hold a grudge, it is noticed; again halting your career in its tracks.

## Quick Tips:

If you don't know, say so! Trying to muddle you way through will show your ineptitude quicker than anything else will.

ALWAYS have your business cards on hand, don't go fetching something that simple, it's like asking for a pen at a contract signing. Be prepared.

## Business – Don't be that...!

When faced with a corporate outing, or gathering. Do not be the one at the open bar getting sloshed and belligerent.

It may be after hours, but your peers will remember and will hold it against you.

For the love of all that is right in this world, use Spell-Check!

Several programs, such as a Thesaurus, a Dictionary, or a Language translator, are already in place for your use!

If your company is small and cannot afford the latest program license, don't worry. The internet is chocked full of free online programs that can help you with all of those things.

Do not think because you had two years of Spanish in High School; that you can converse to a Spanish-speaking supplier.

The plain and simple truth is, YOU CAN'T! Get help, use a translating program or a Spanish to English dictionary. Anything is better than taking a guess at it. Grammatical errors in any language is not nice.

Don't be that person who only offers "What-ifs" during a meeting or presentation.

What you are being presented or shown during a meeting is broad scoped information. Take it as that and if you have any questions, follow-up with them afterwards, send an e-mail, swing by their office

Or ask your boss if you don't fully get it, explain what you didn't understand, and see if they can help. They may be as confused as you are, together you can get the correct information, and clarify the situation.

If it is your meeting, never be afraid to stop the tirade of 'what-if' situations from your peers.

Bringing them back on topic, will get more of your goals accomplished. As long as you are professional about it, being the level head in the room, sets you apart.

# Cursing – What is proper

Proper cursing, is there such a thing? Sure, we are people and bound to use our vocabulary as such. There are times when a firm 'Damn it' can feel great and help to expel frustrations. Again, with anything that is somewhat naughty, less is more.

If you are the person who never gets upset, a well placed 'shit' could emphasize your way to respect. Adversely if you throw the 'F-bomb' around like it is a normal salutation, you will lose all creditability, almost immediately.

## Saying no, the right way

Saying no can be difficult, especially if you are trying to make a name for yourself in the corporate world.

There is a way you can say it without tarnishing your reputation. Instead of saying, "No way you're piling anything else on me!" instead try to divert the assignment.

Ask questions about deadline, and scope of the project. If it is something, you can squeeze out in five minutes when you get time, take it. If it will require a large dedication of your time, talk it out with your manager. Let them know what you are currently working on, and let them make the choice.

You will feel better, and your boss will understand your capabilities. Both are beneficial, and remember that if you are a part of the solution, you cannot be the cause of the problem.

## Nepotism – It's real, you have to cope

Nepotism happens, and you can never know when it is going to rear its ugly head. Nepotism is definitely unpredictable, one minute you are on top of the world with a successful project. The next minute, you are screwed over and the new hire gets the promotion.

Example: The brand new guy is best friends with the boss, and he got the job! Yep, it happens, sorry to be the bearer of bad news.

It is not fair or right and it is definitely not the way to go about daily business. However, that is the boss' deal, not yours. You have to realize that in today's society, no one is exempt from this major nuisance.

You have to come to terms with the following statement; it is difficult, but live by the words. "You cannot get upset over the things you have no control over!"

Take it on the chin, and move on. This person cannot take every promotion, so wait your turn.

Either the "Golden Child" will live up to the expectations or they won't." If they do make it, give credit where credit is due.

If they don't make it, don't gloat. Be the person who picks up the pieces, you will end up with an

apology for not being chosen,
and a promotion.

Remember positivity wins out,
every time.

# Learning –The ins and outs of Corporate College!

If you do not have a degree, it does not mean you should not be constantly learning. We all have our reasons why we did not continue our education. They are valid reasons, mostly. You know who you are, again don't lie to yourself!

However, your status, nor financial strength, should ever stop you from learning. Even if it is something as simple as picking up a newspaper; being up to date and in the 'know' are all examples of learning.

Learning should never stop even if you cannot afford College; so many companies offer online courses and/or training. Do not be afraid to sign up for them, most are generally free, and/or some companies also provide cost offsets, or reimbursements.

These trainings or classes can be listed on your resume', take credit for everything even if it was something as simple as basic ledger balancing. This would equate to basic accounting and potentially give you future education credits.

Each class or training you take counts as being interested in your career, and bettering yourself as a person.

The balancing act; you have a major project or deadline on your plate, an upcoming class or meeting ends up throwing a major monkey wrench and changes your day into chaos.

Now you cannot miss the class, since your boss signed you up for it. No way, do you not go?

Not the case, the business world can be more flexible than you may believe. If your deadline is major, ask your boss.

Remind them of your prior educational commitments, if it is an important class, they can move your deadline. Not an important class; they will get you on board for a private class, or in the next session.

Remember learning is important, but do not think you are working

somewhere just for their classes.
You still have a job to do.

## Office Programs – Have fun don't worry

Do not rely on your audience being as in tune with technology, as you are. The simplest program to you could be foreign and alien to others.

Make sure that each and every presentation you create, is readable to anyone who could potentially be in attendance.

If you are that person who does not know the difference between a database, and a spreadsheet, learn! Keep learning especially if it is a program that allows you do your job better.

Your peers will help you, and most companies understand that not every new employee has knowledge or experience with all programs. They will teach you, you just have to voice your willingness to learn.

If you are the tech savvy guru, shine and share. Yes, share your expertise suggest a program, or macro that could help someone.

If you are the helper/teacher you will be looked at as a key contributor. Which can help you become more integrated into your company and the cross functional teams, that make up our corporate world.

The last few tidbits:

Family and work, we have been there! You are in an important meeting and your spouse knows it. However, there they are on the phone calling in. What do you do?

They are not stupid, something is wrong at home. Politely excuse yourself, apologizing as you go. Step out and take the call.

No way can that be appropriate!

Wrong, most professionals understand there is family involved. Things happen, things we may never see coming.

Now conversely never take the call while in the meeting, or talk to your friends for half an hour, because this part of the meeting does not involve you. Bottom line, you are only as professional as your outer appearance, if you appear to be non-committal, and indifferent to your role. You are probably close to losing it.

. . . . . . . . . . . . . . . . . . . . . . . . . . . . . . . . . . . . . . . . . . . . . . . . . . . . . . . . . . . . . . . . . .

We hope you enjoyed this, and that it was helpful to you, remember to keep learning. The only message, which we hope you follow, is to do the right thing.

Whatever you hose up now, even if you aren't caught; can rear its ugly head in the future. Be responsible, and save yourself the headache, no matter what the problem, most issues can be resolved without much trouble at all.

Please remember, skating by and getting one over, never works. Karma is a bitch and does not miss a thing.

We wish you all the best, and remember...

"Don't get upset over the things you can't control!"